This Coloring Book Belongs to:

_____

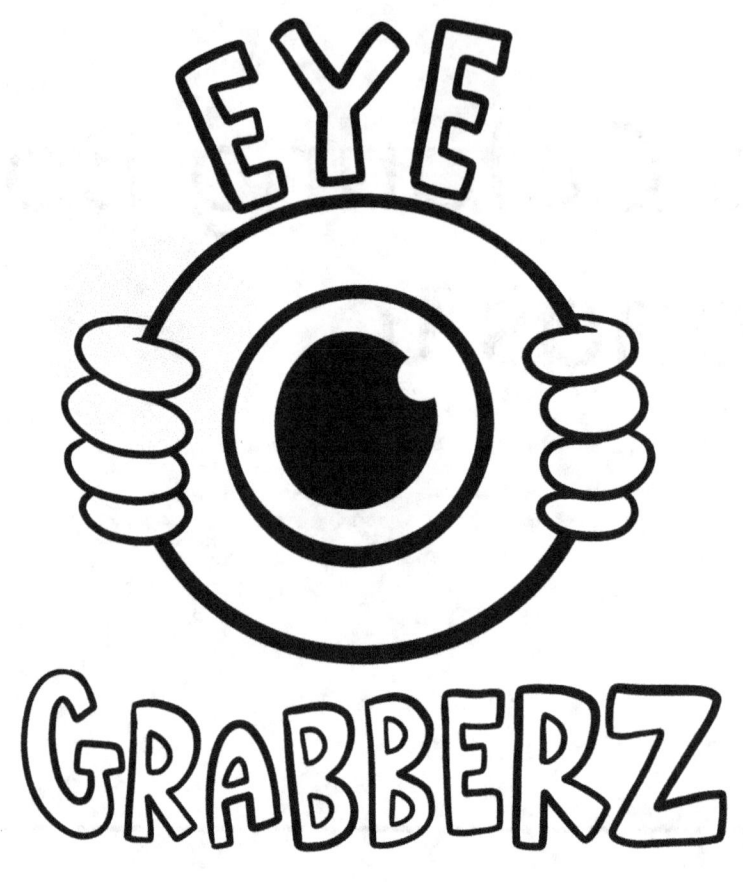

Copyright 2020 Eye Grabberz Books

www.eyegrabberz.com

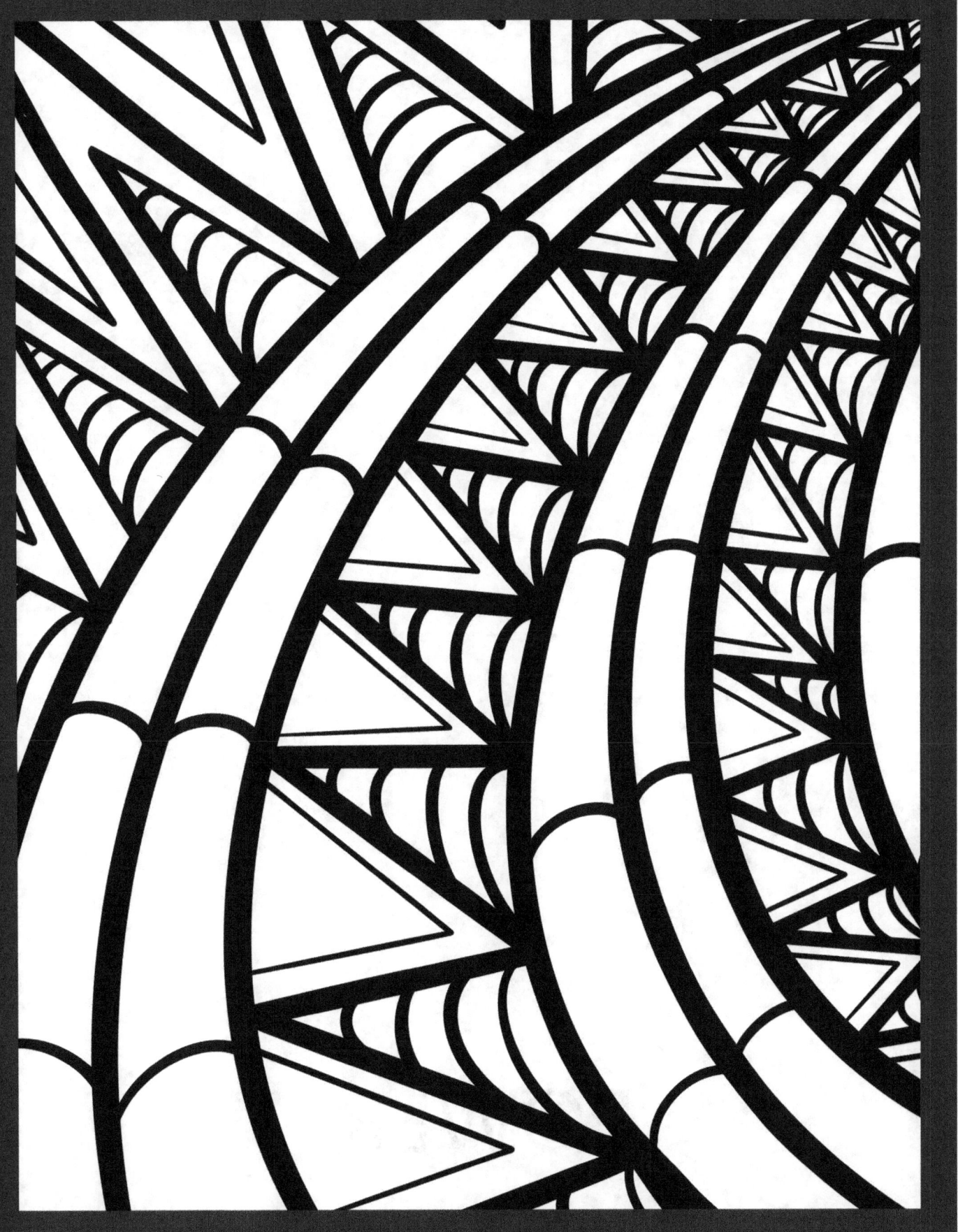

POWER

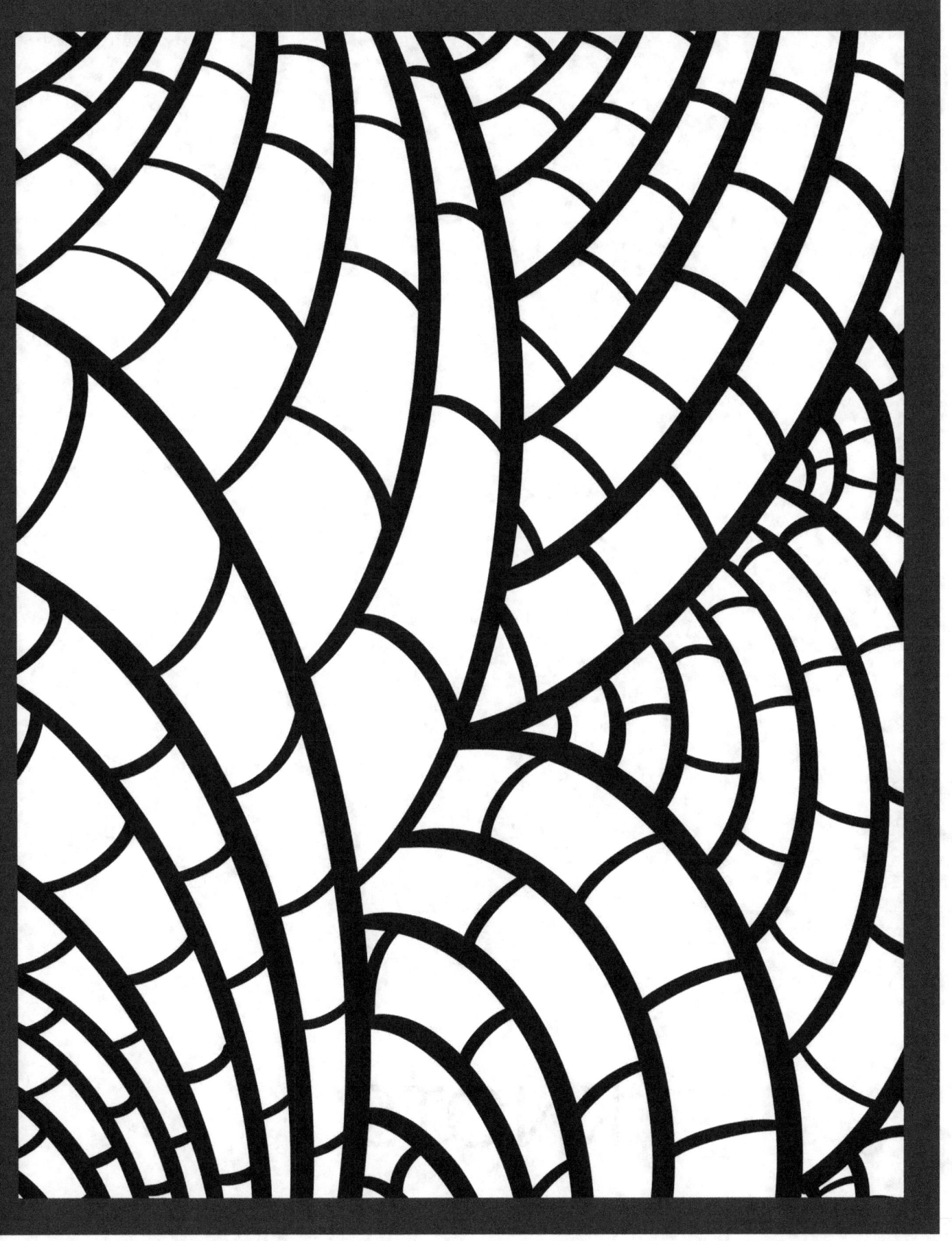

KNOTS

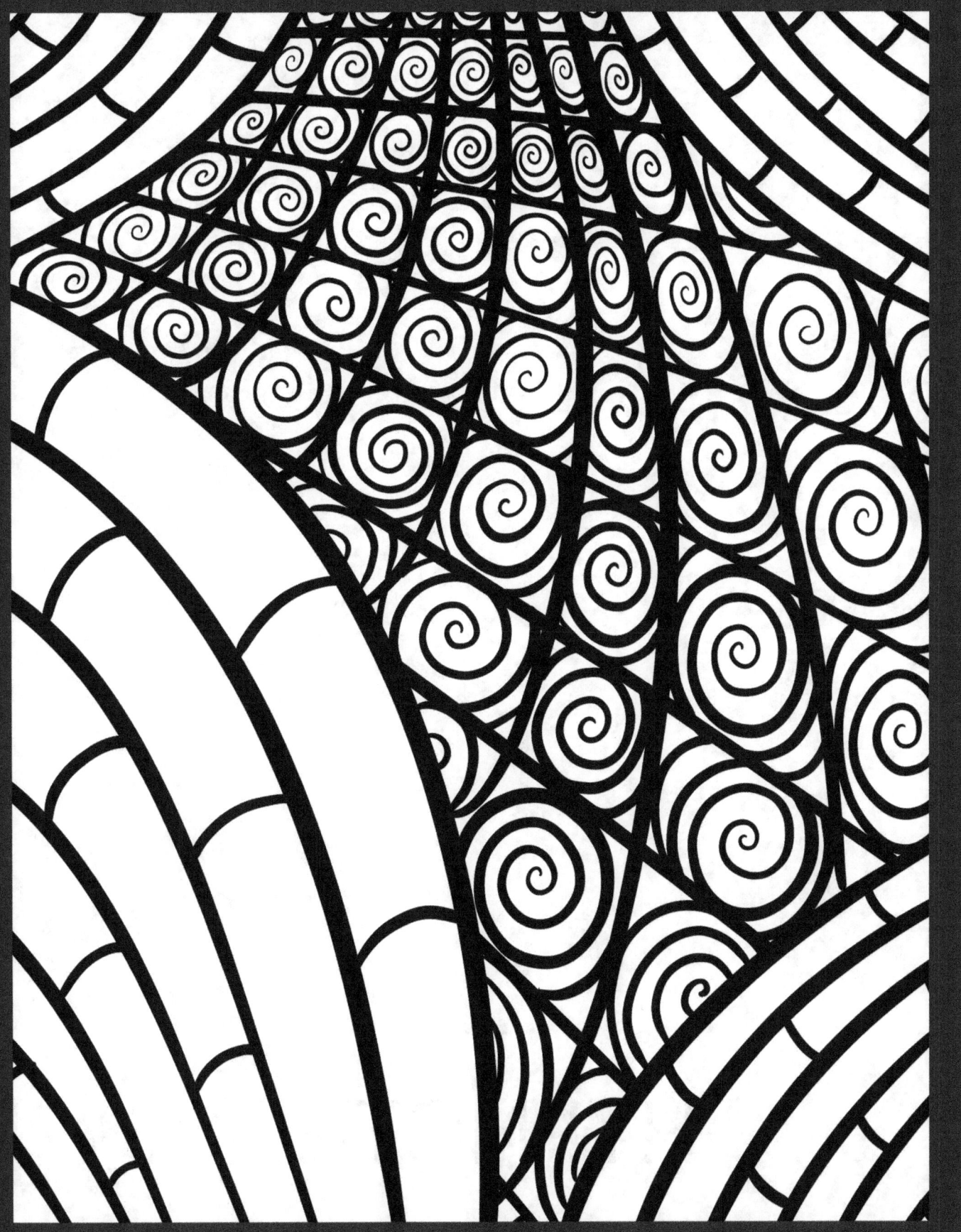

HYPNOTIC

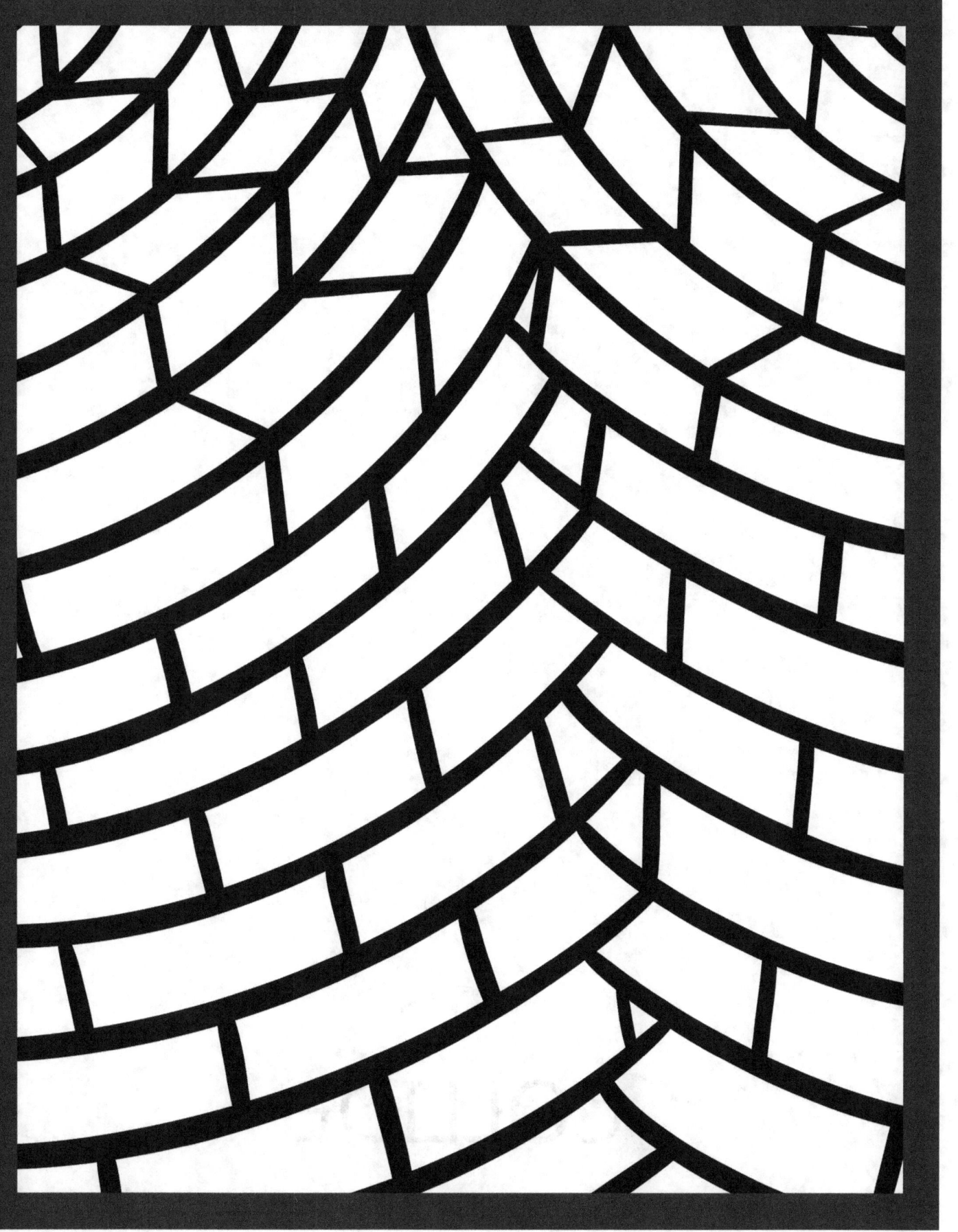

COLLIDE

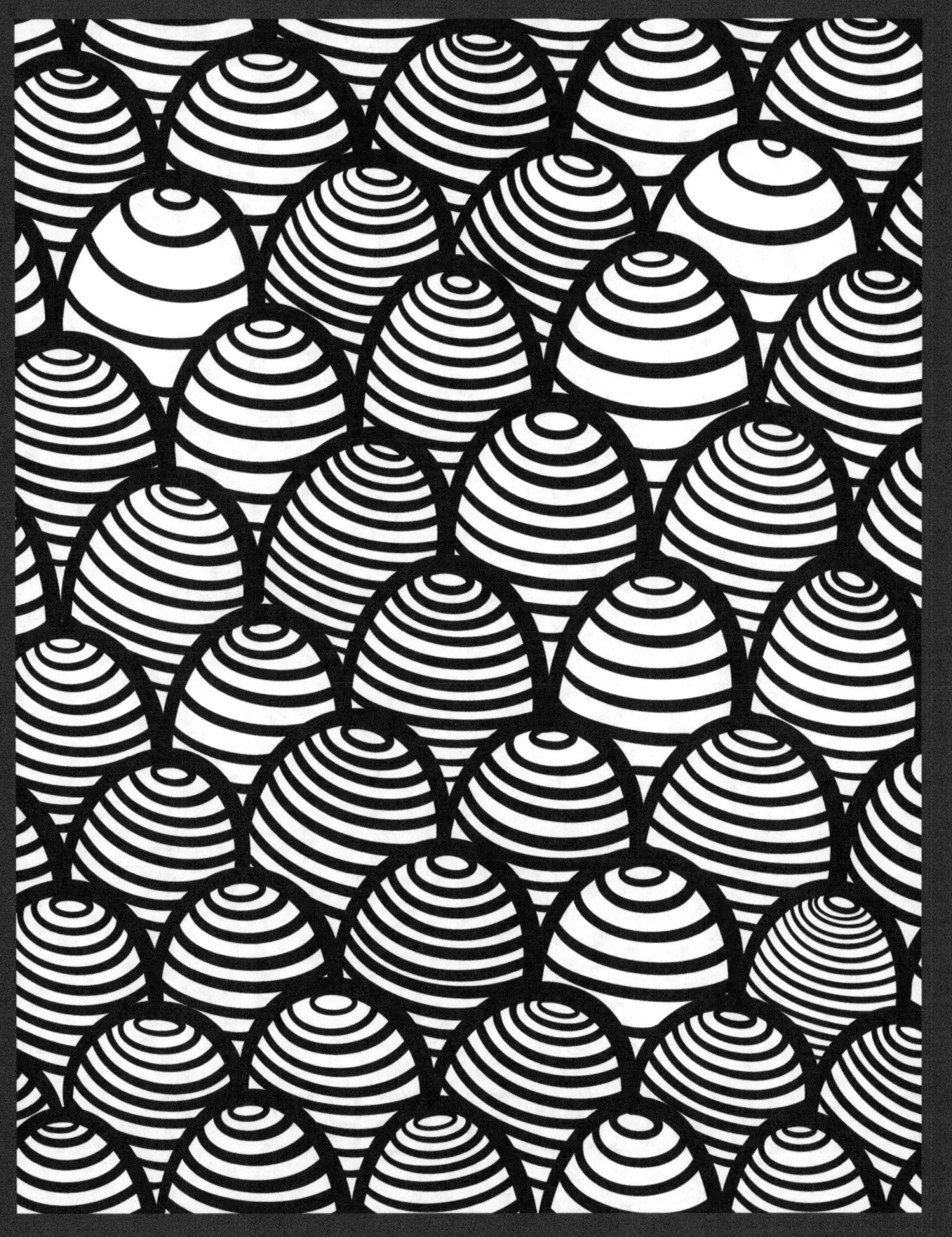

OUTLIERS

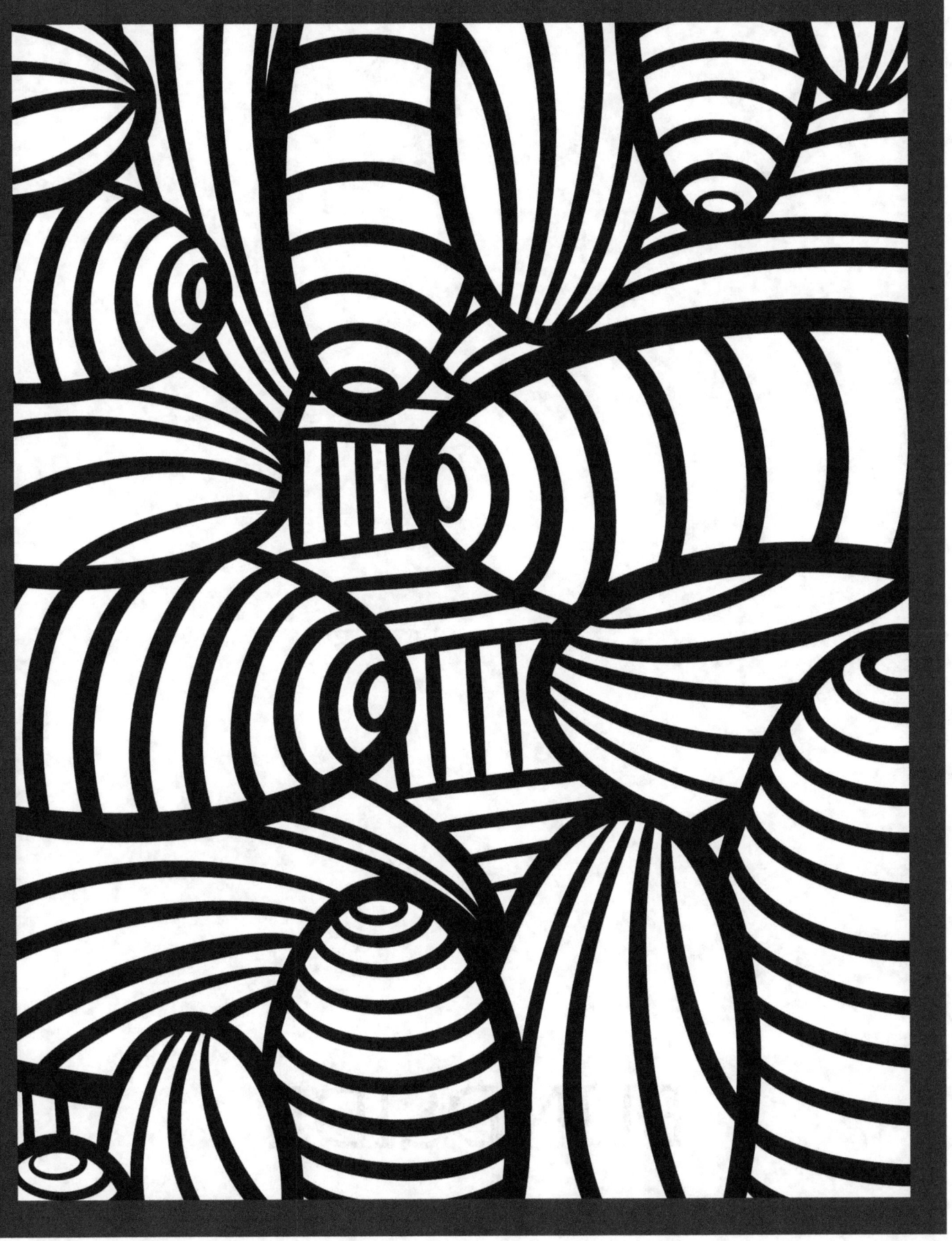

BLINDSIDE

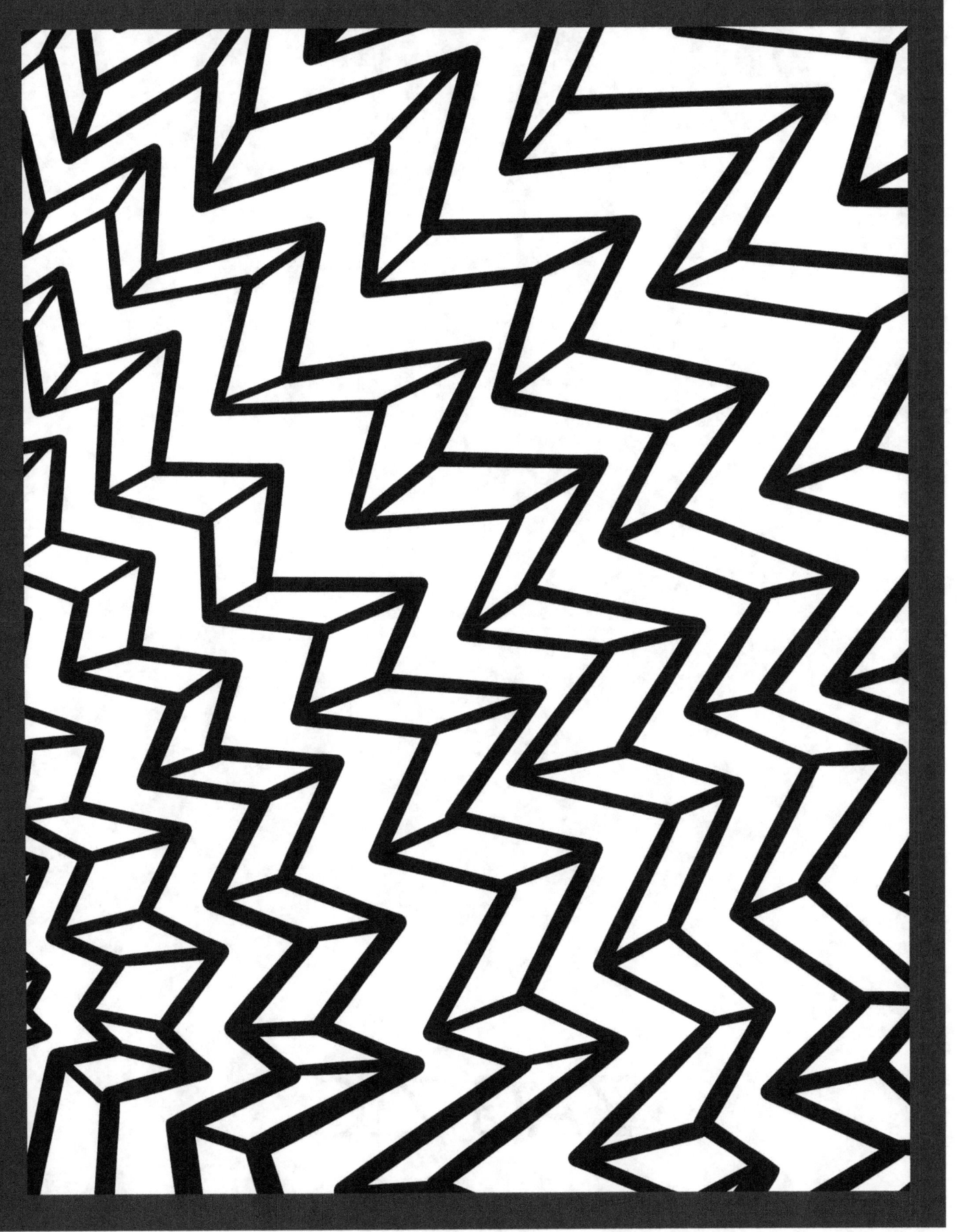

ZAG ZIG

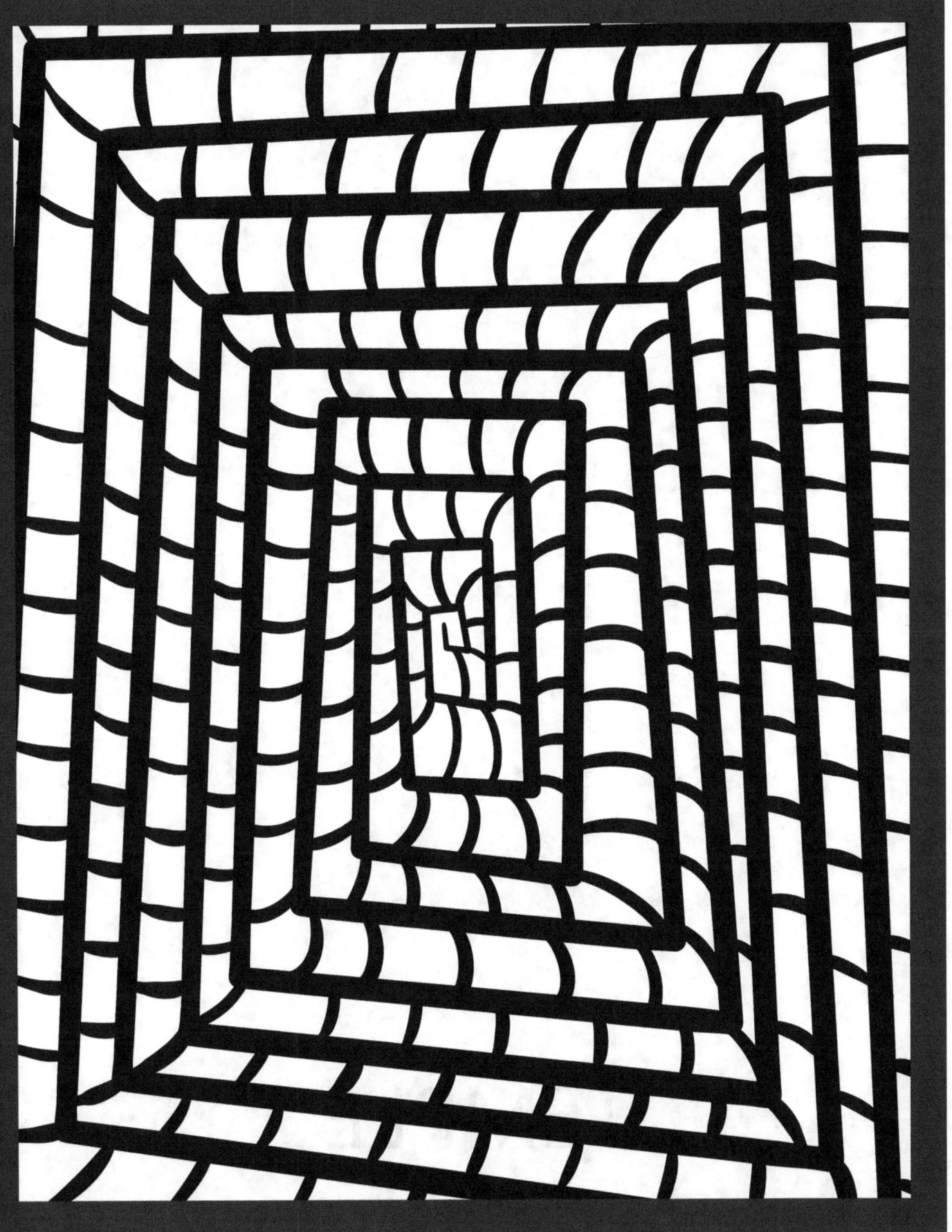

TEMPLE

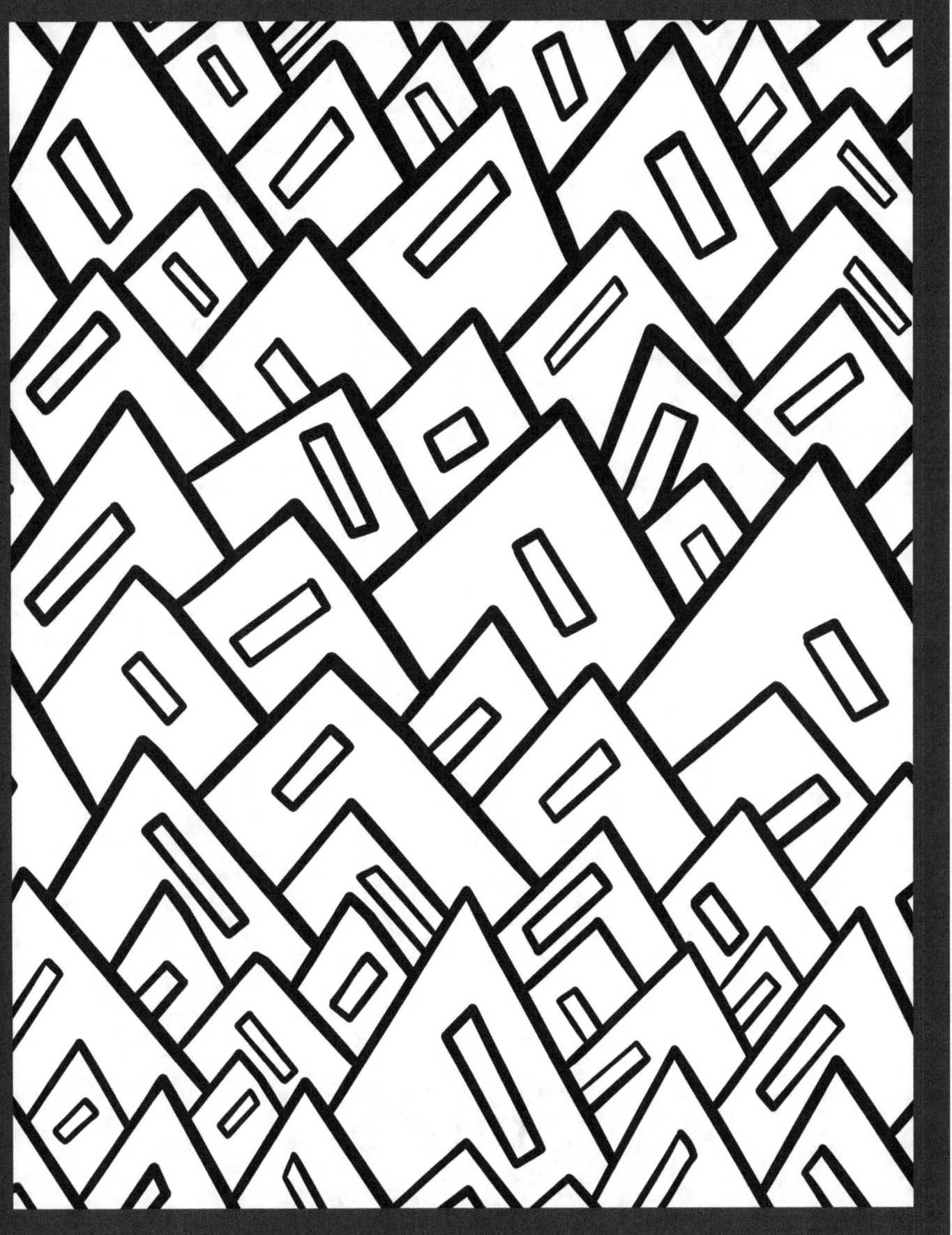

CHIPS

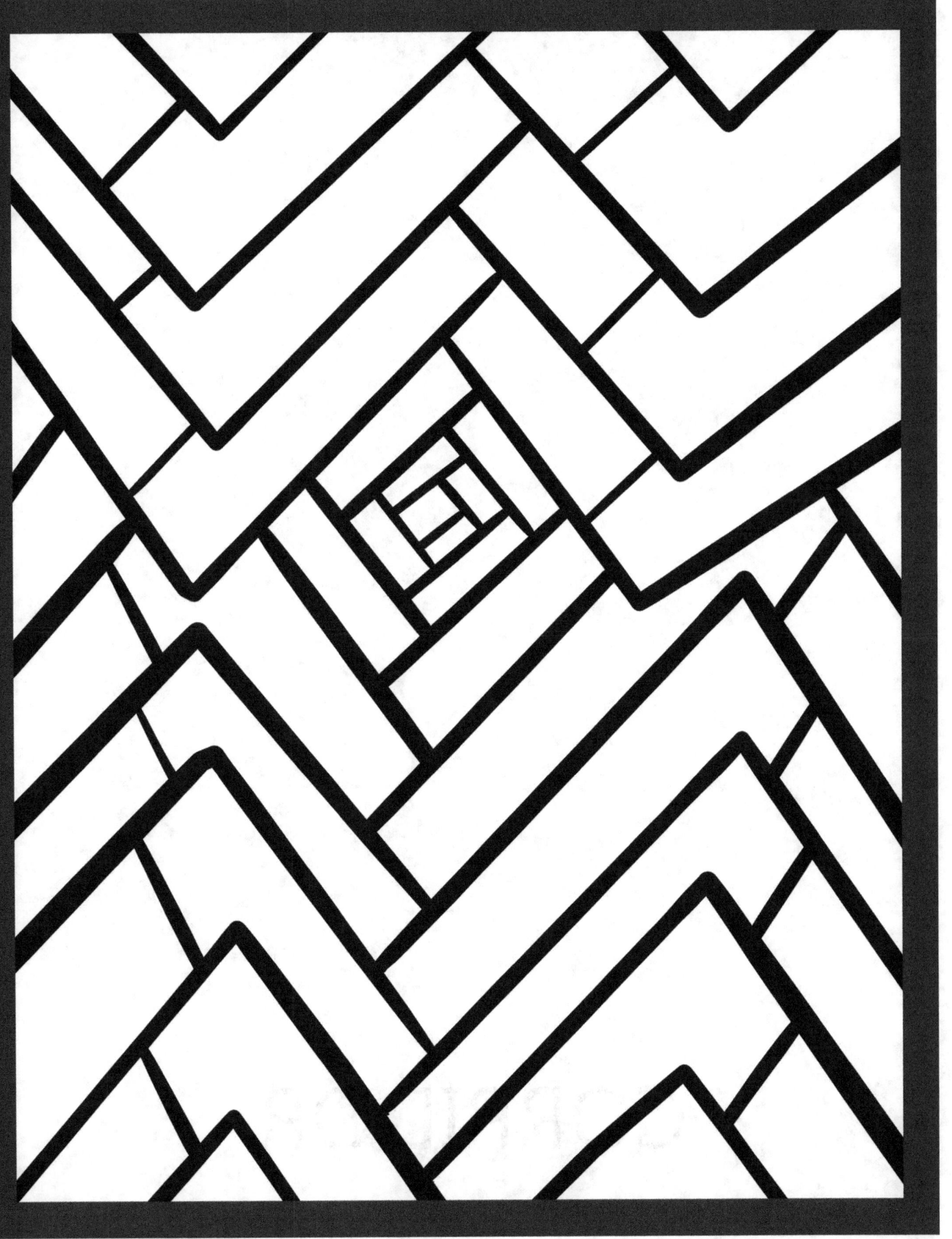

CORRIDOR

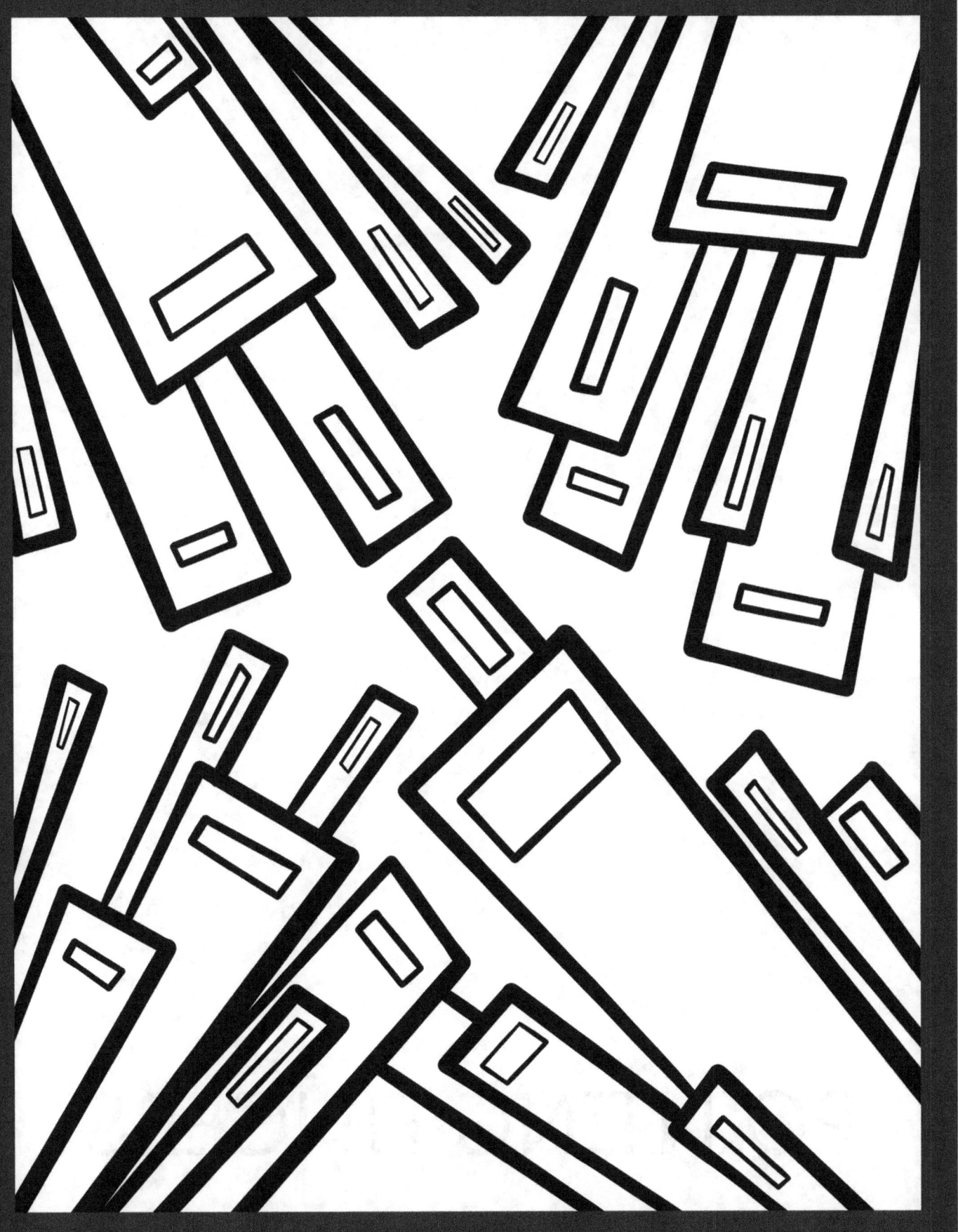

POINTING FINGERS

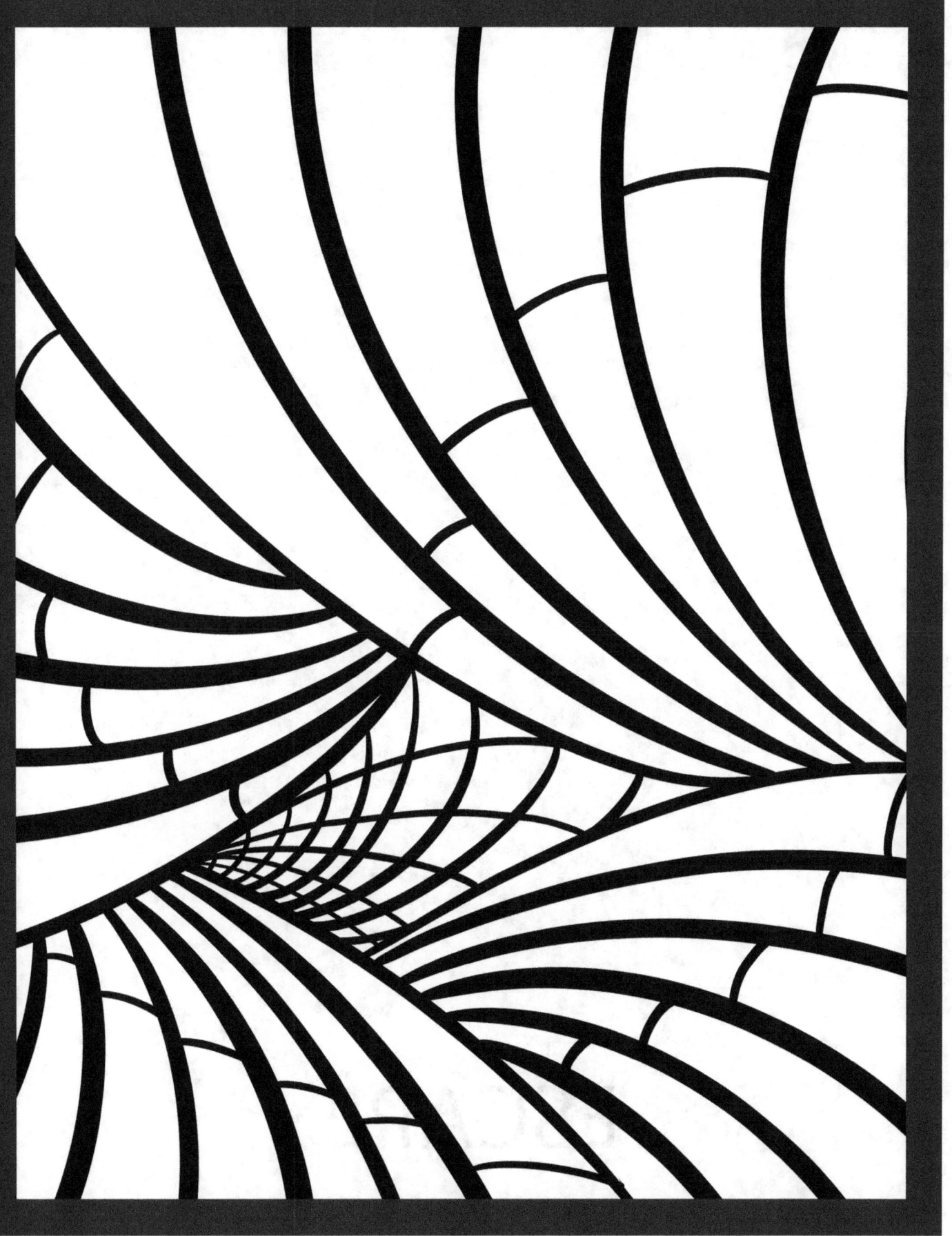

ESCAPE

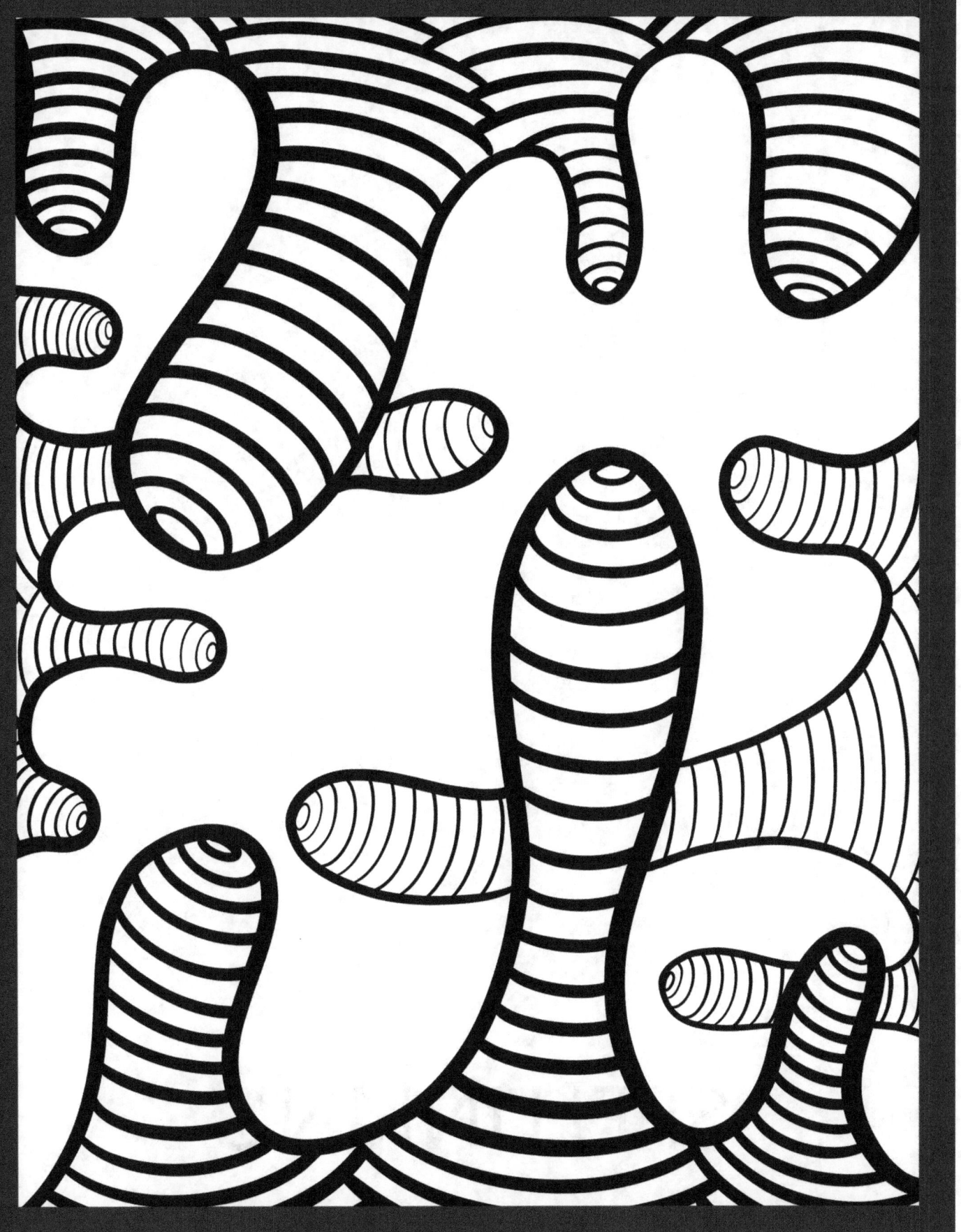

SPELUNKING

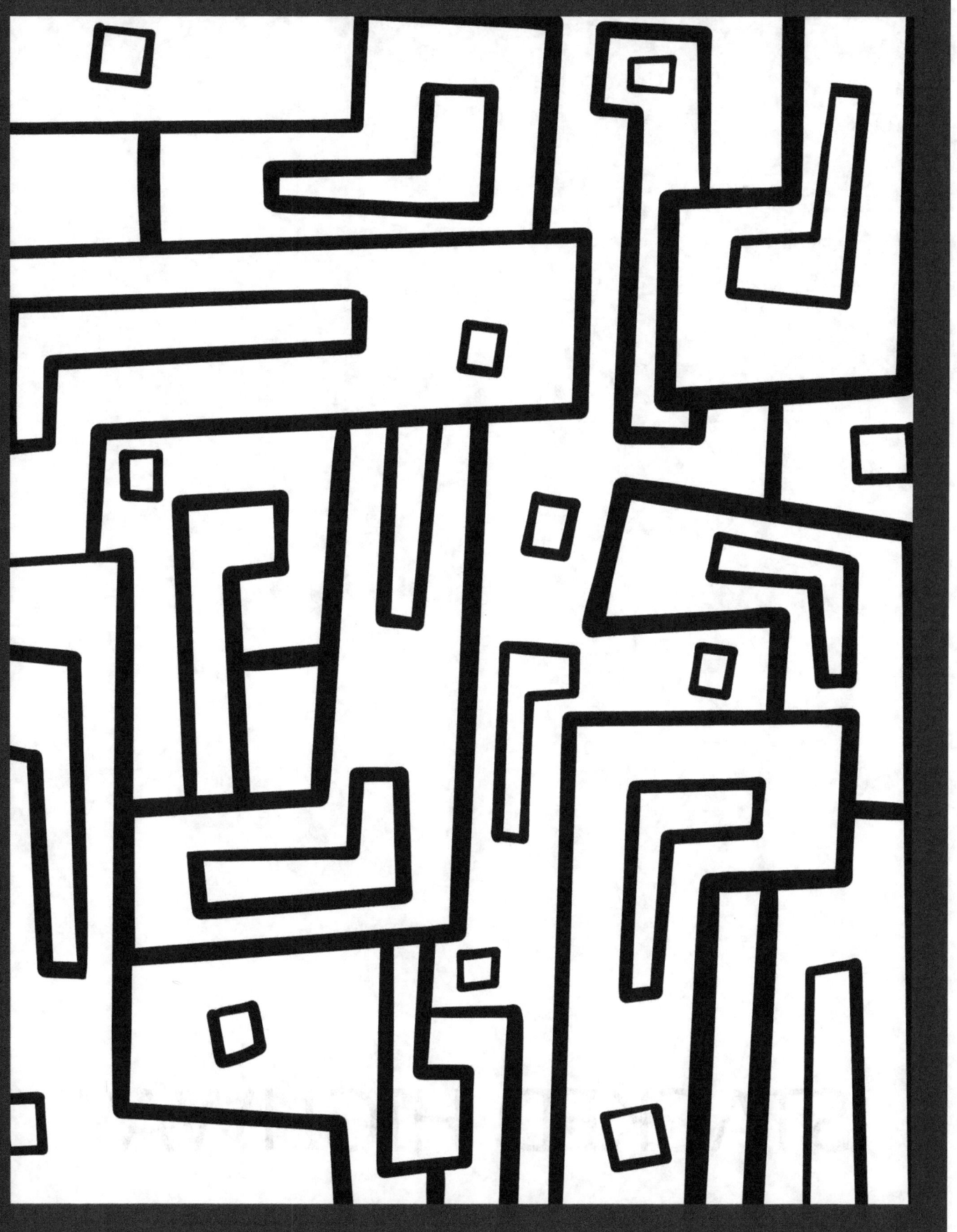

stacked highway

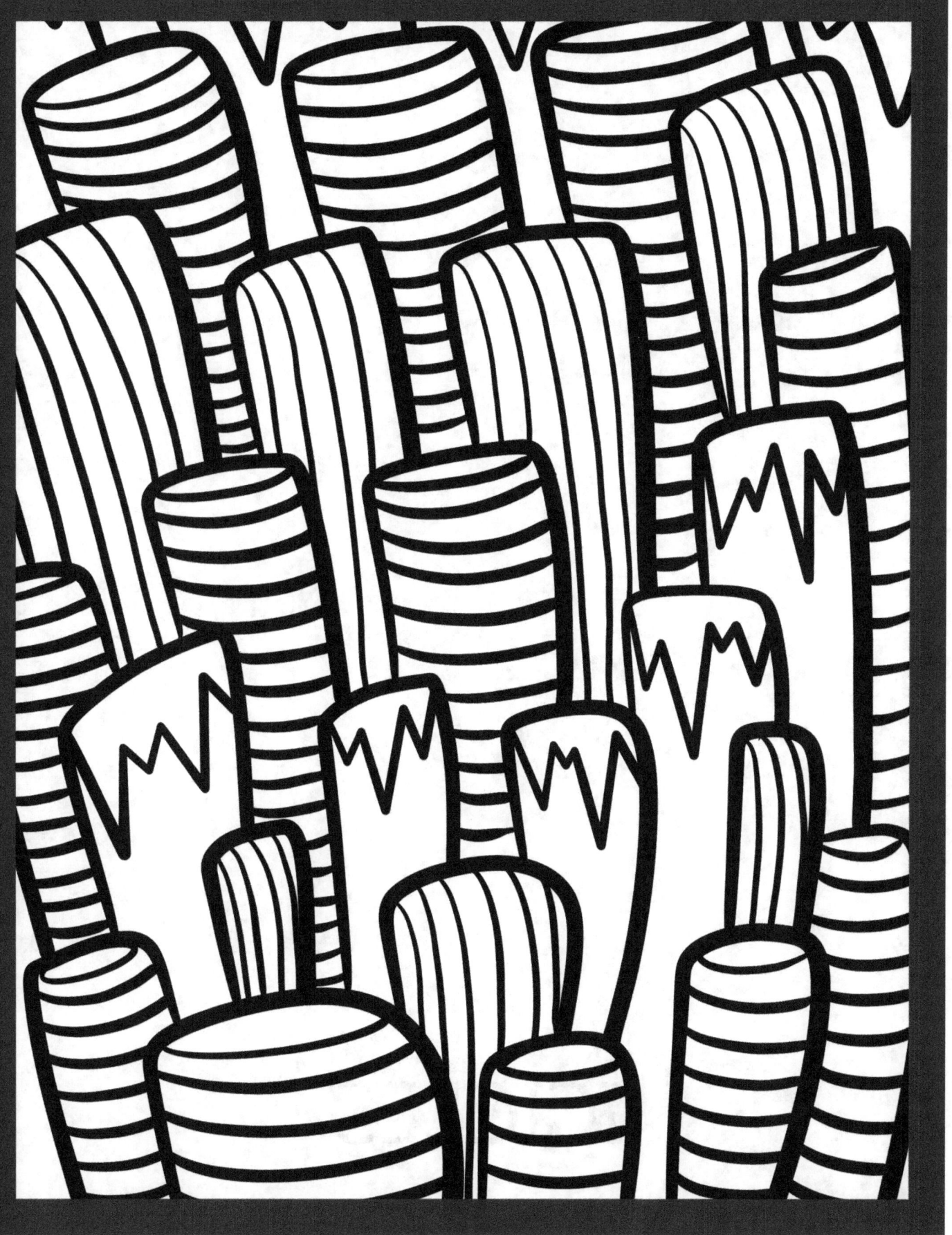

ICICLES

CHAIRS

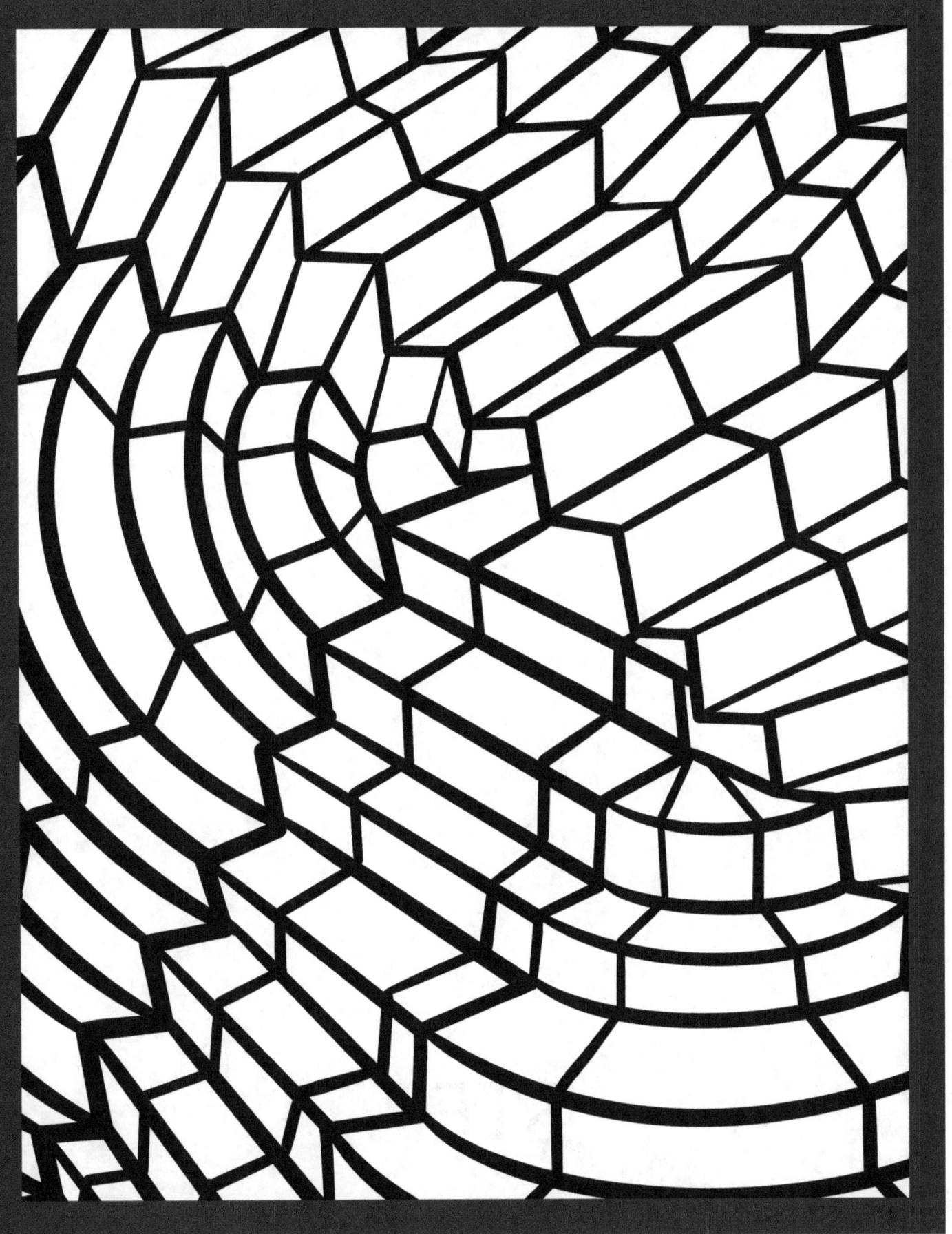

STEP

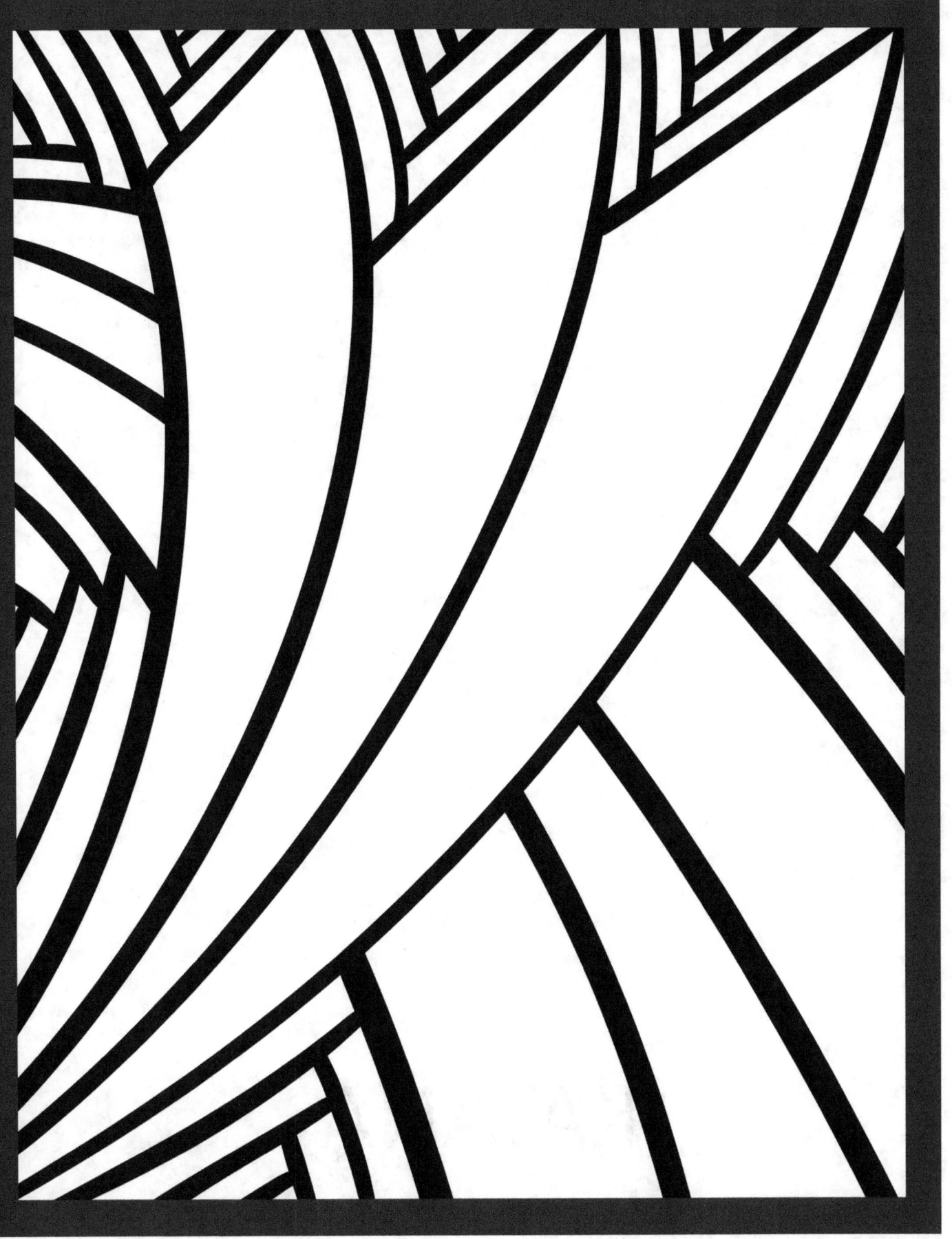

KATANA

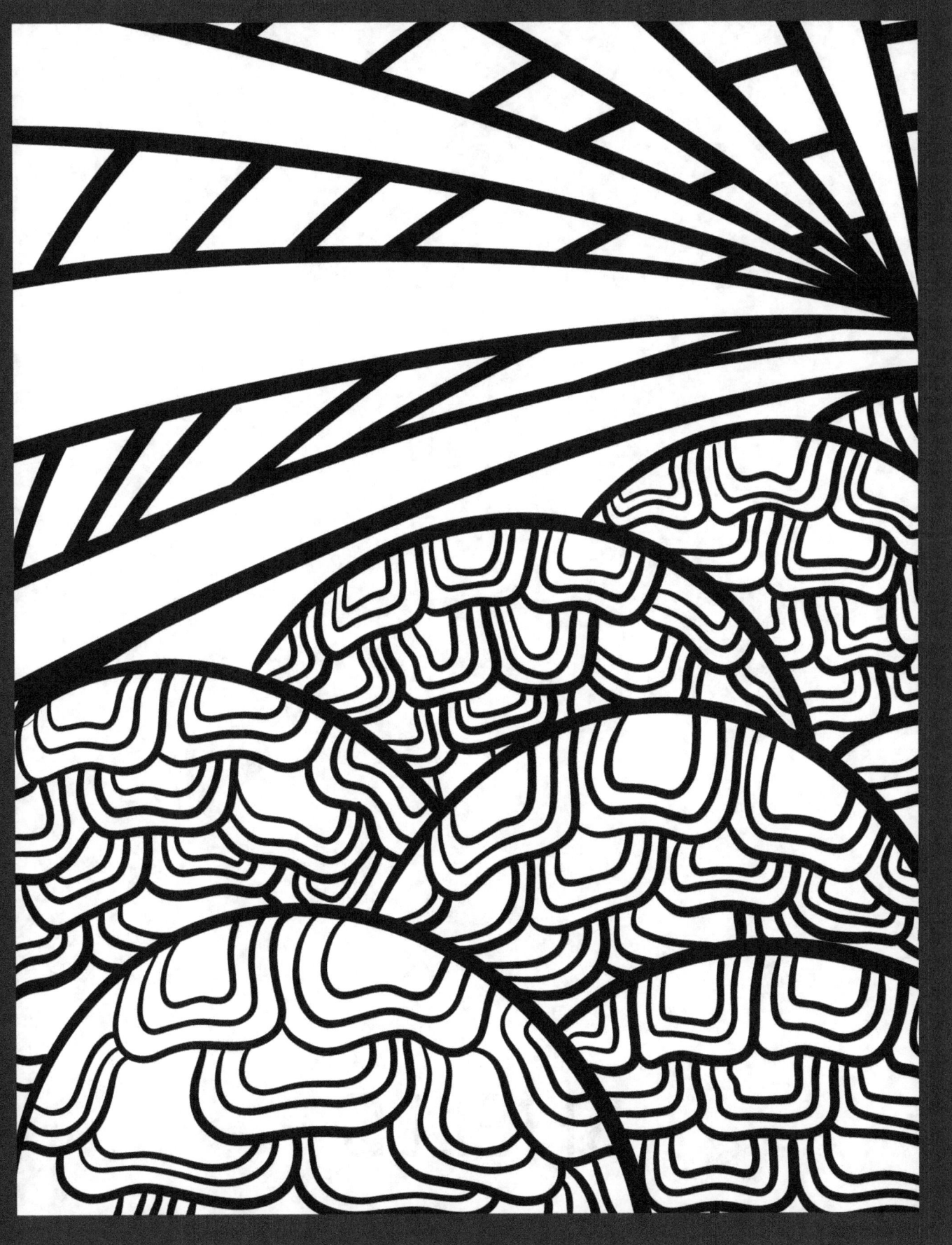

SHELLS

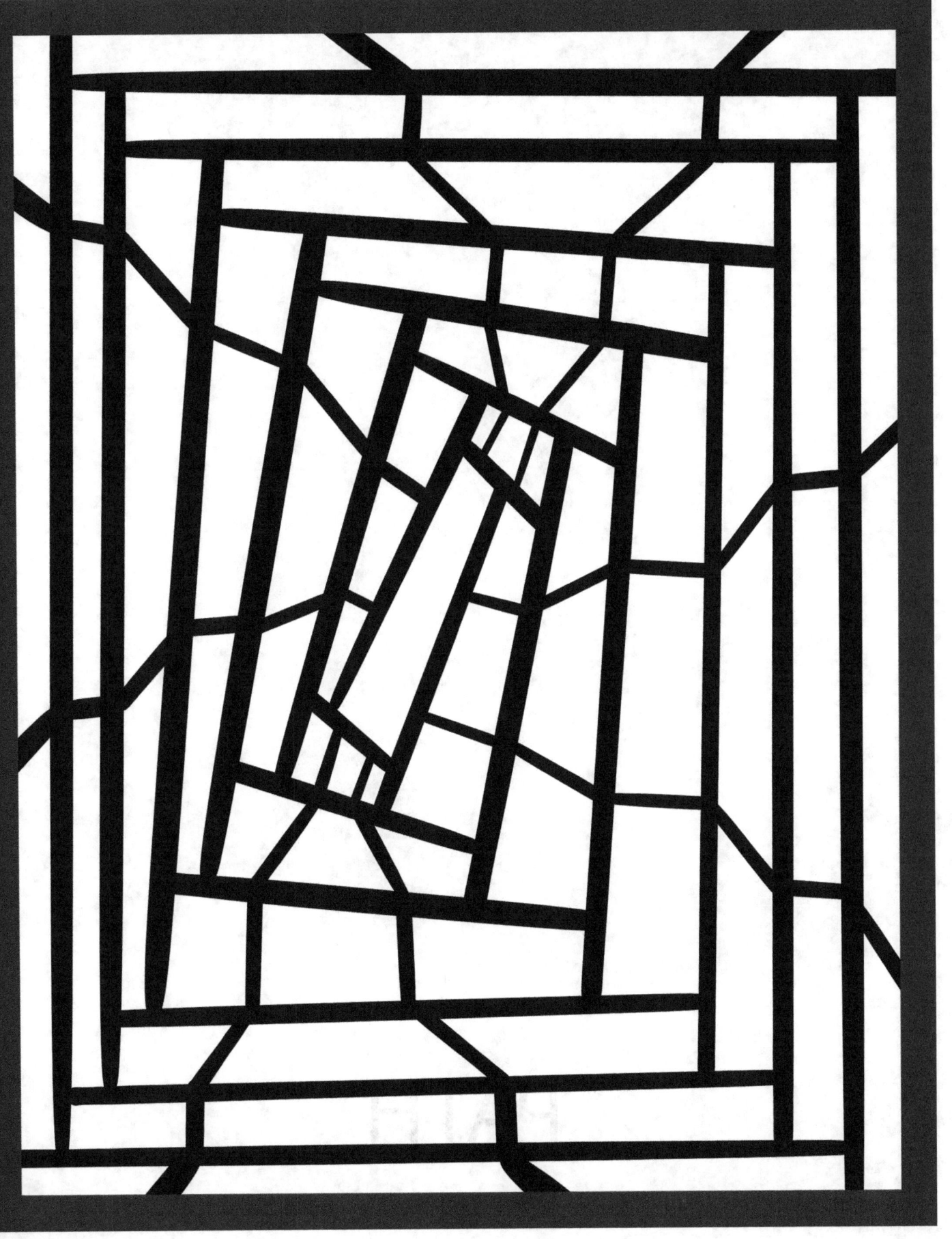

PATH

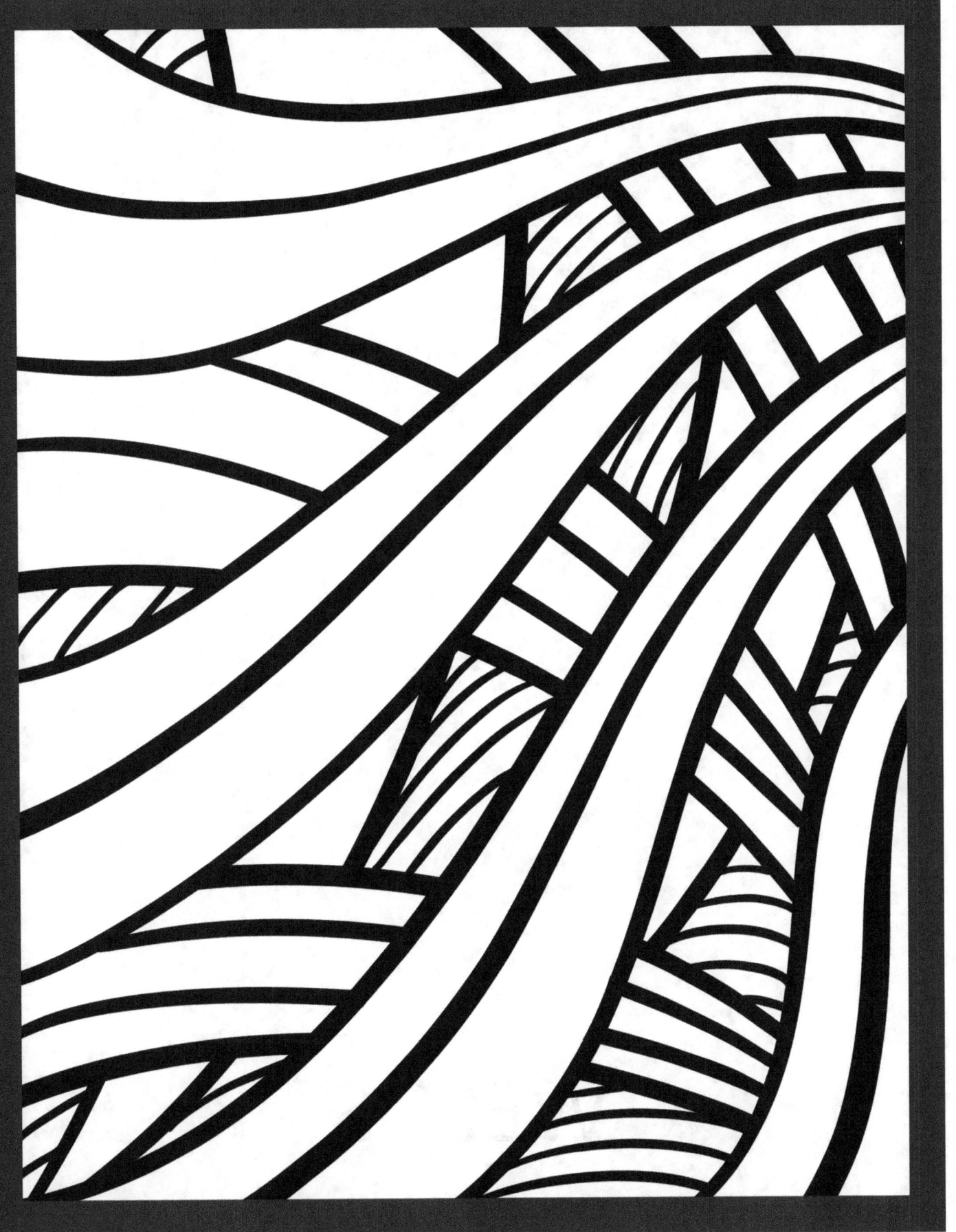

WEEDS

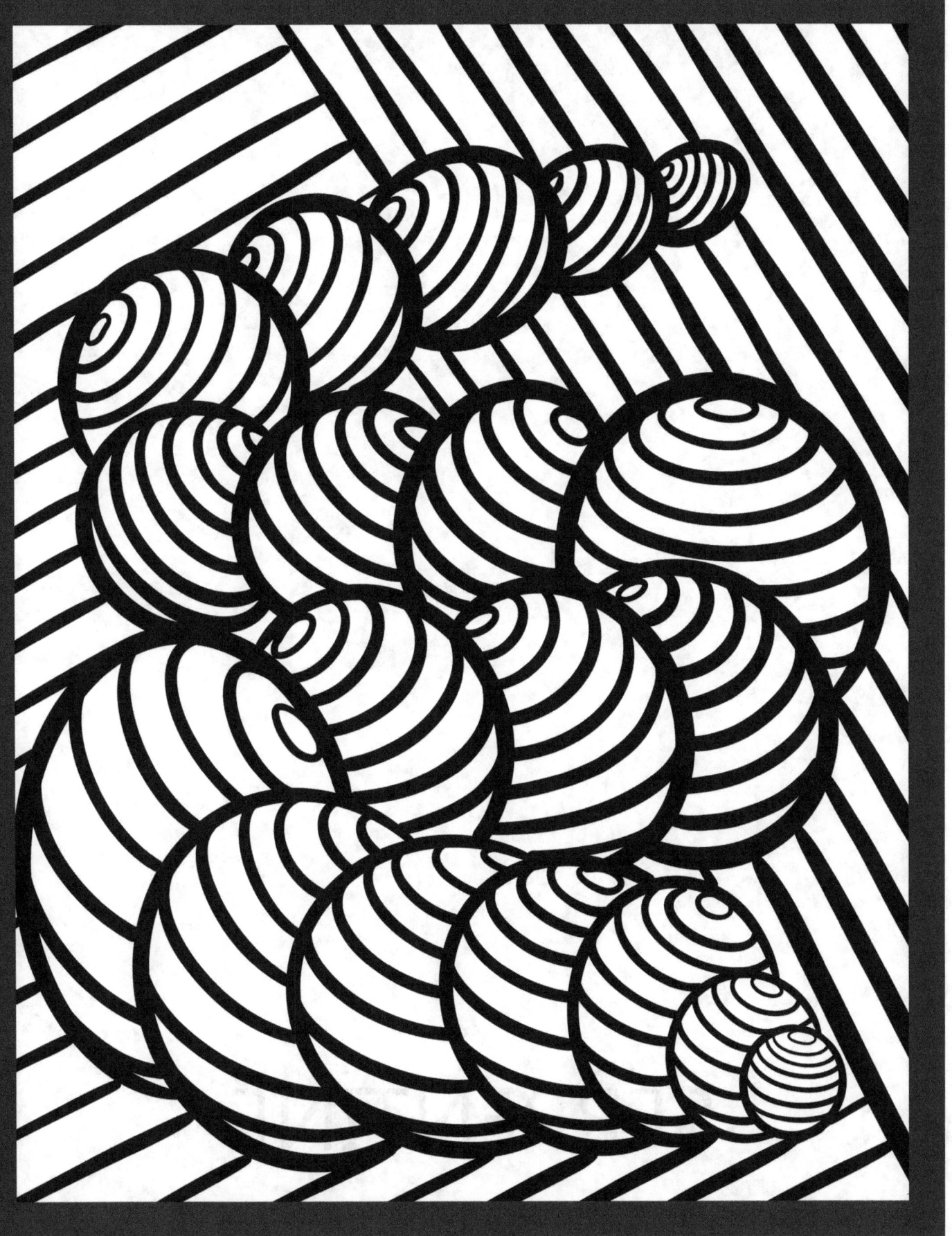

SERPENTINE

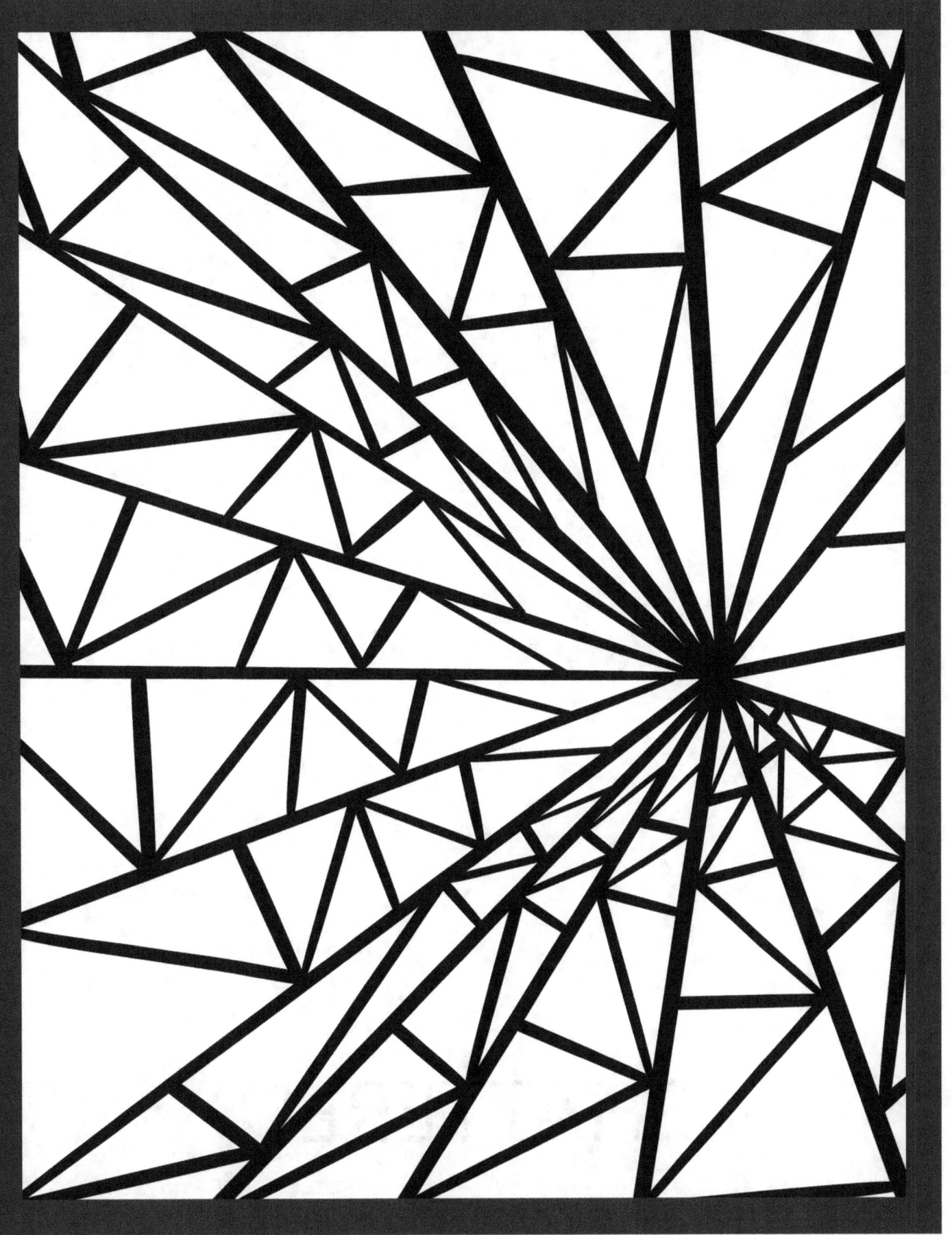

SHATTERED

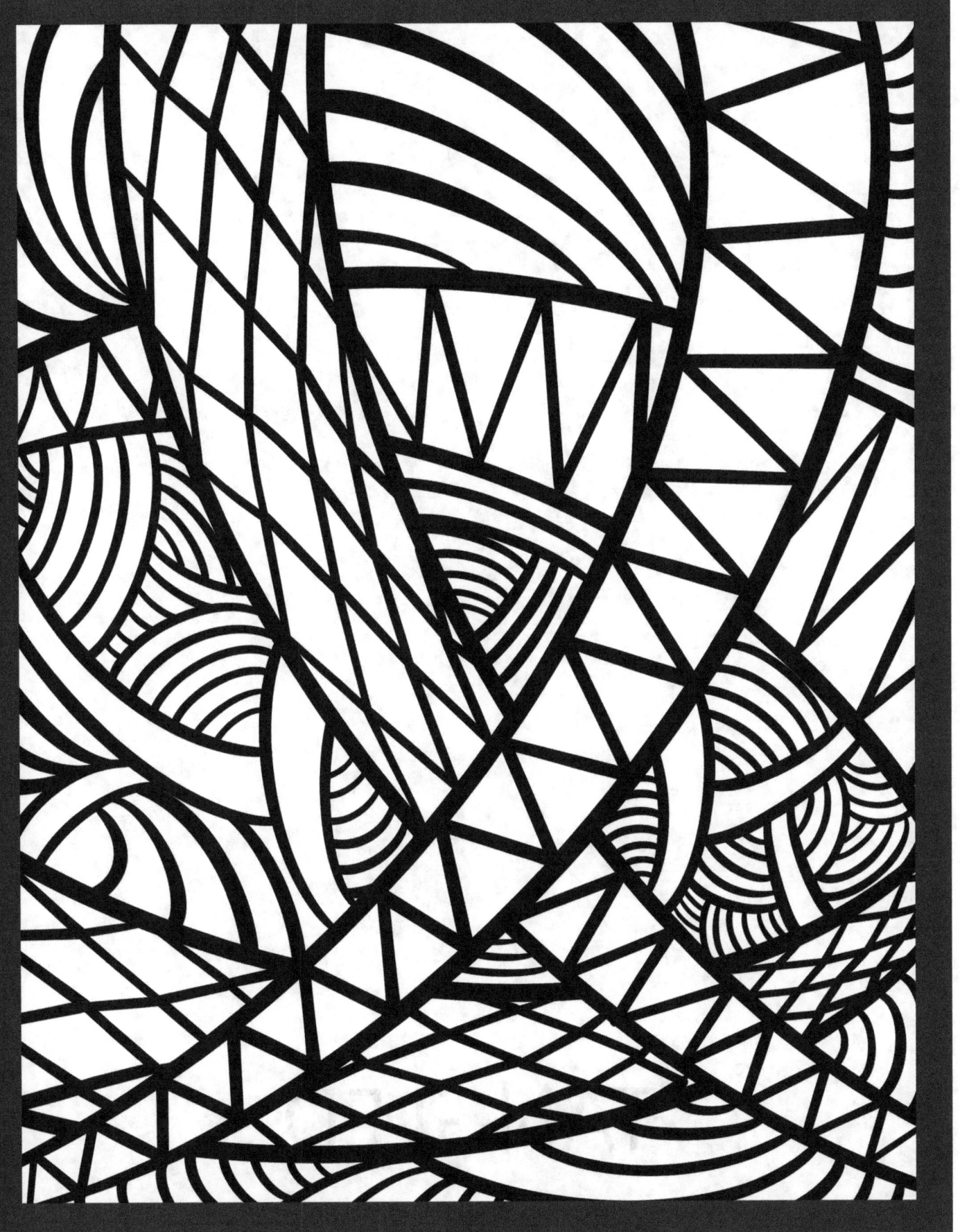

TANGLED

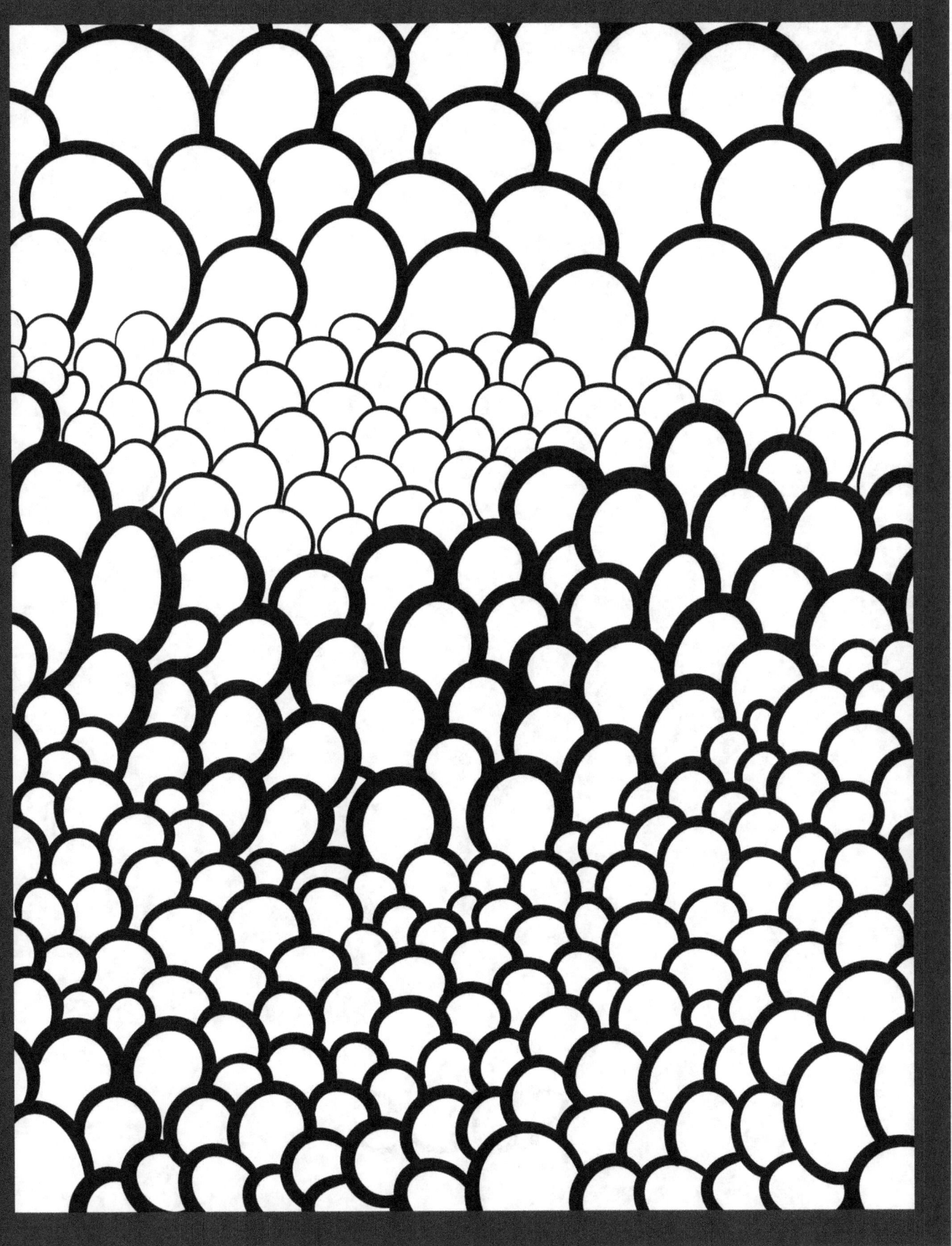

SUDS

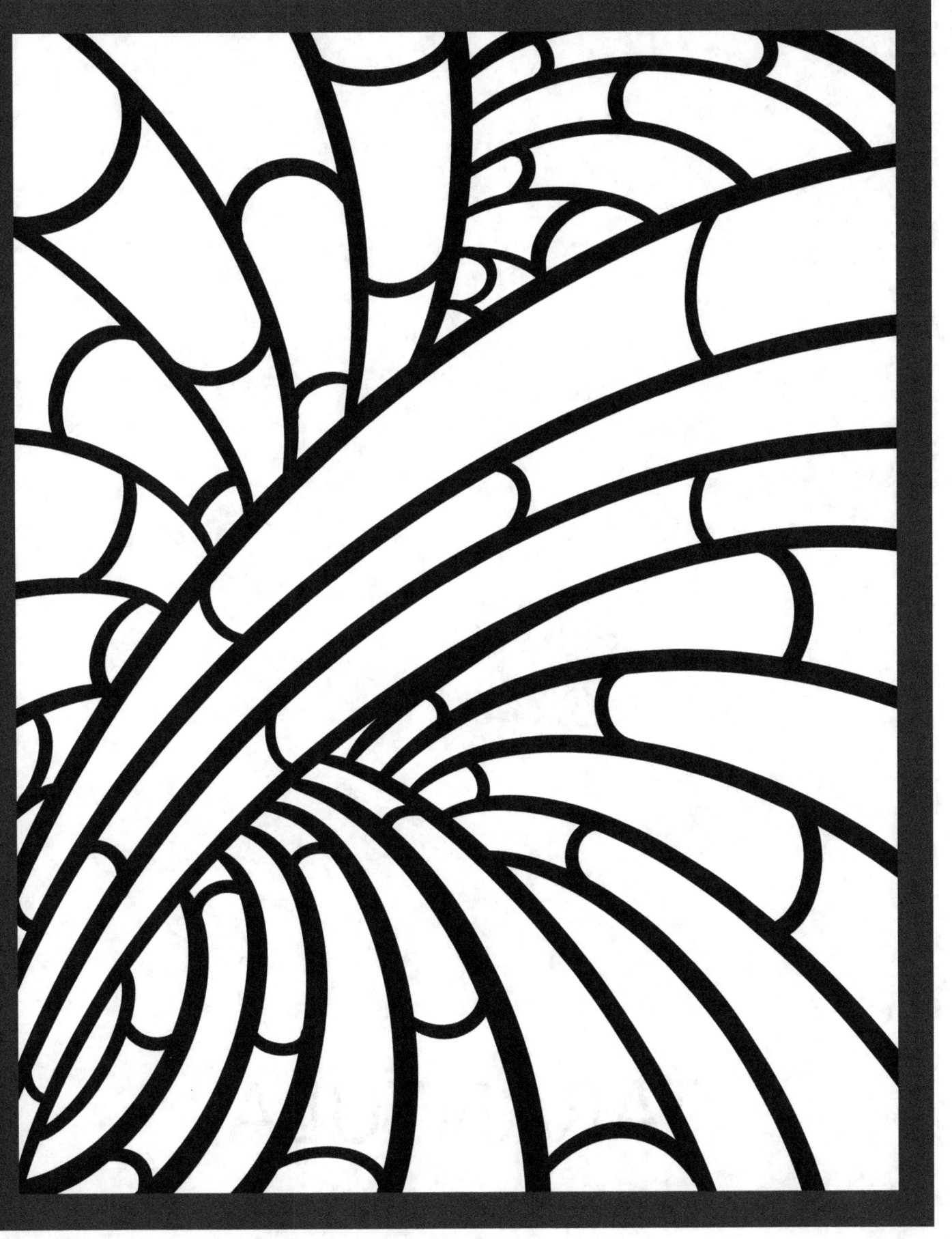

TARANTULA

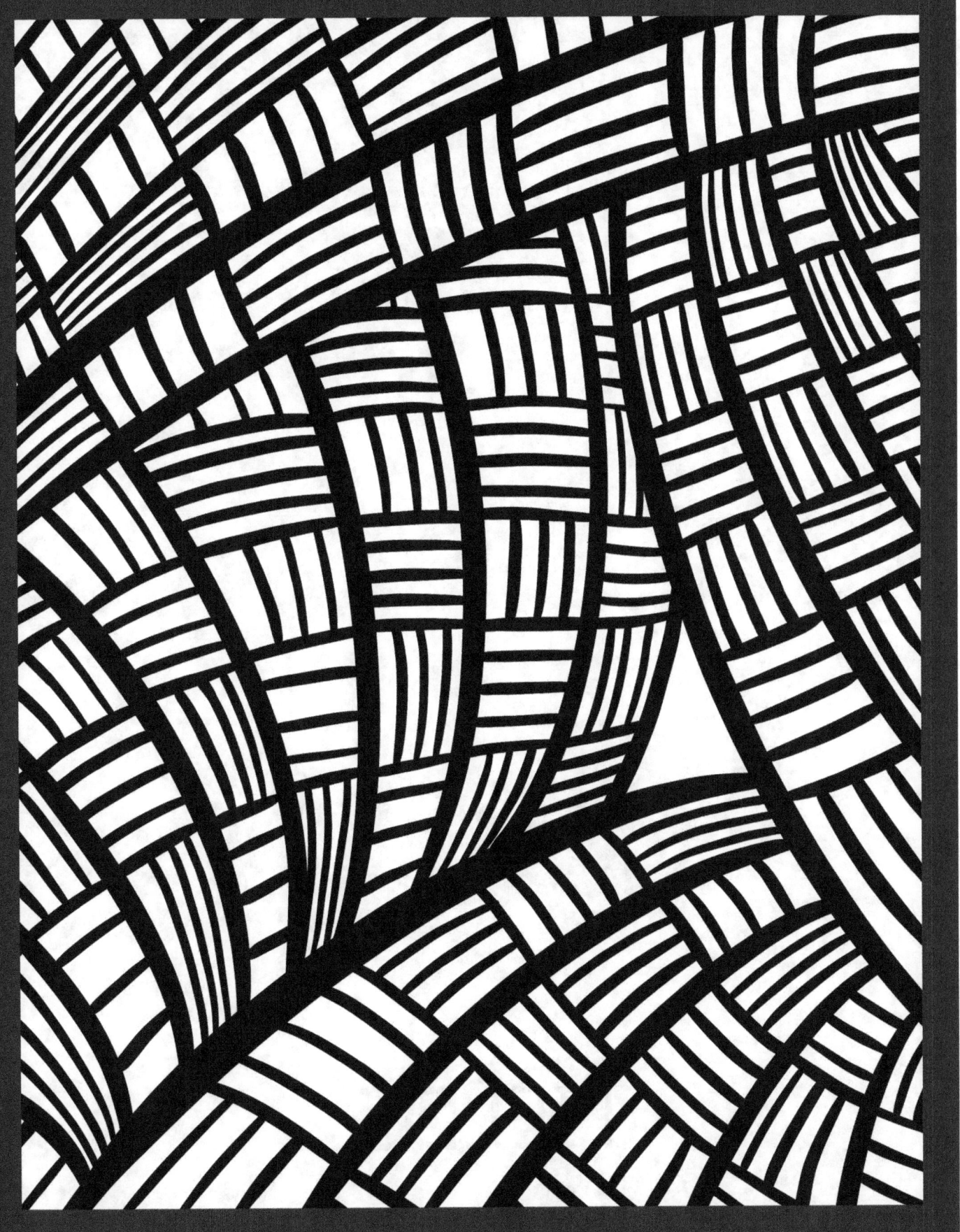

FIELDS

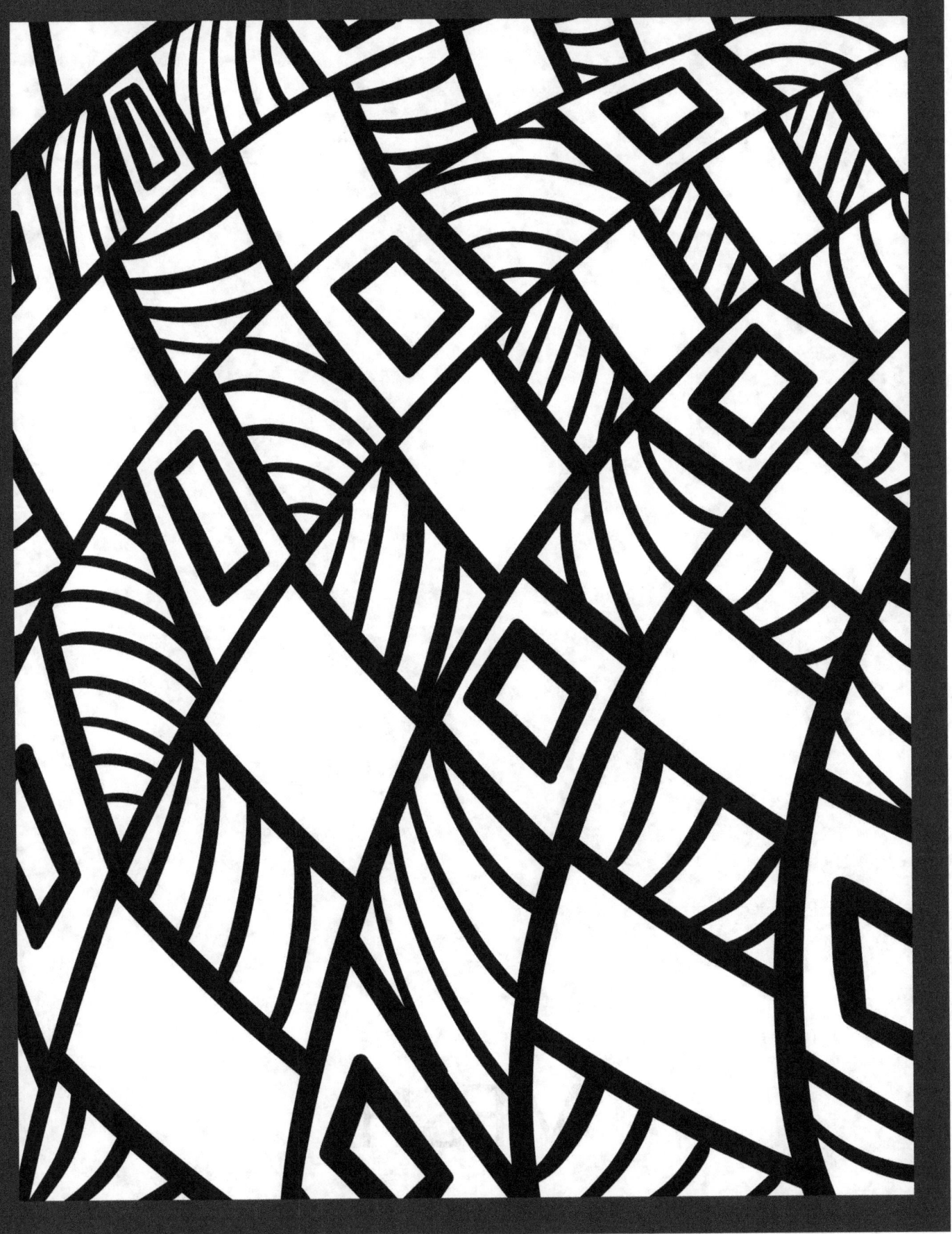

MESH

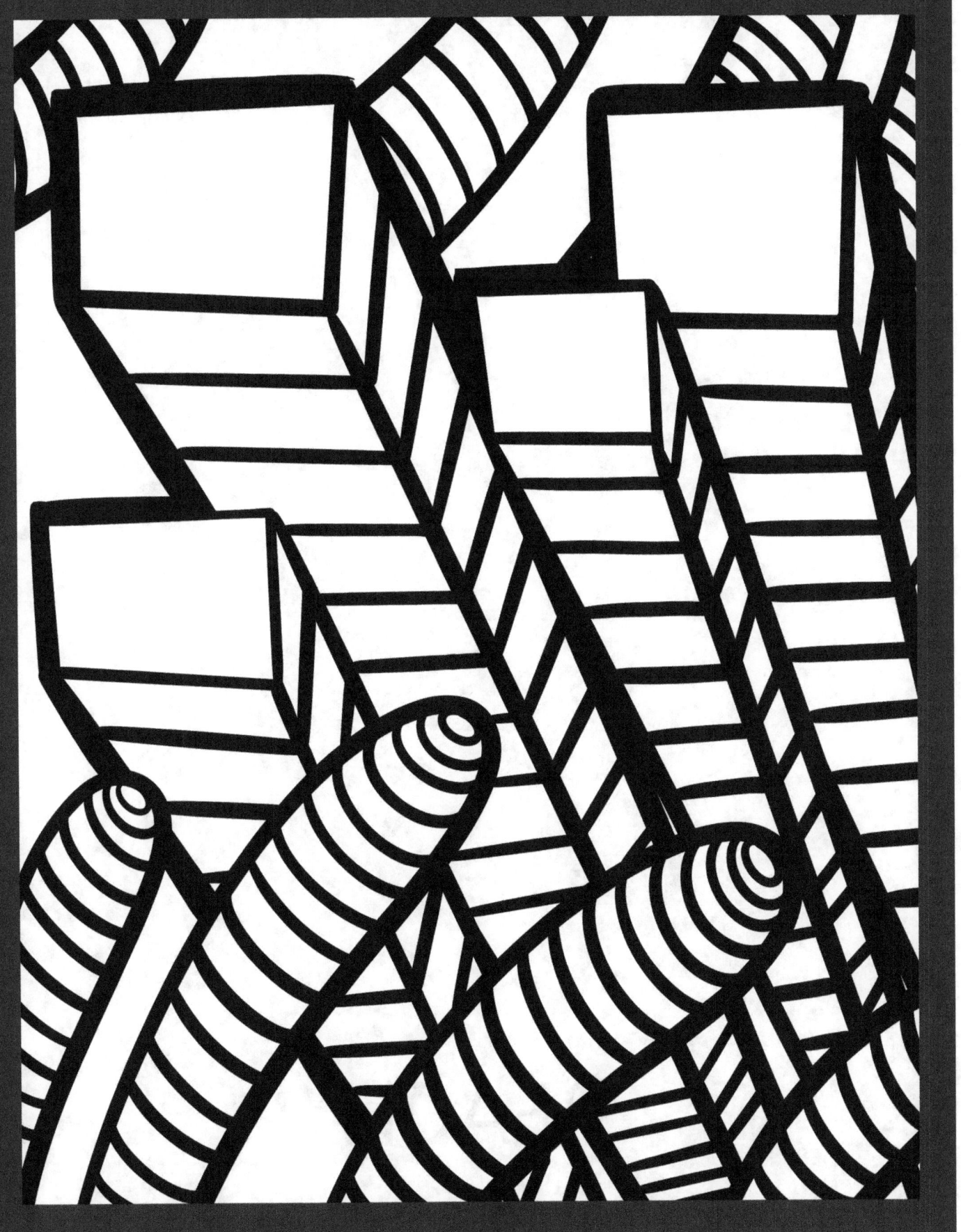

REACH

WIDGETS

www.ingramcontent.com/pod-product-compliance
Lightning Source LLC
Chambersburg PA
CBHW080528220526
45465CB00006B/2635